CEDAR MILL
COMMUNITY LIBRARY
12505 NW CORNELL RD.
PORTLAND, OR 97229
503-644-0043
W9-BYH-449
WITHDRAWN
CEDAR MILL LIBRARY

OUR EARTH

Written and illustrated by

ANNE ROCKWELL

VOYAGER BOOKS
HARCOURT, INC.
Orlando Austin New York San Diego London

Our earth is where I live.

It is a big, round globe.

It has a frozen North Pole at the top
and an icy cold South Pole at the bottom.

Our earth was shaped by water, fire, ice,
and living things. It is always changing—
much too slowly for us to see.

Once our earth was covered with warm water.
Some dinosaurs lived in its warm and ferny swamps.
Then our earth turned cold.

Huge sheets of slowly moving ice called glaciers crept across the earth and wore rocks smooth. Glaciers are still moving in places on our earth.

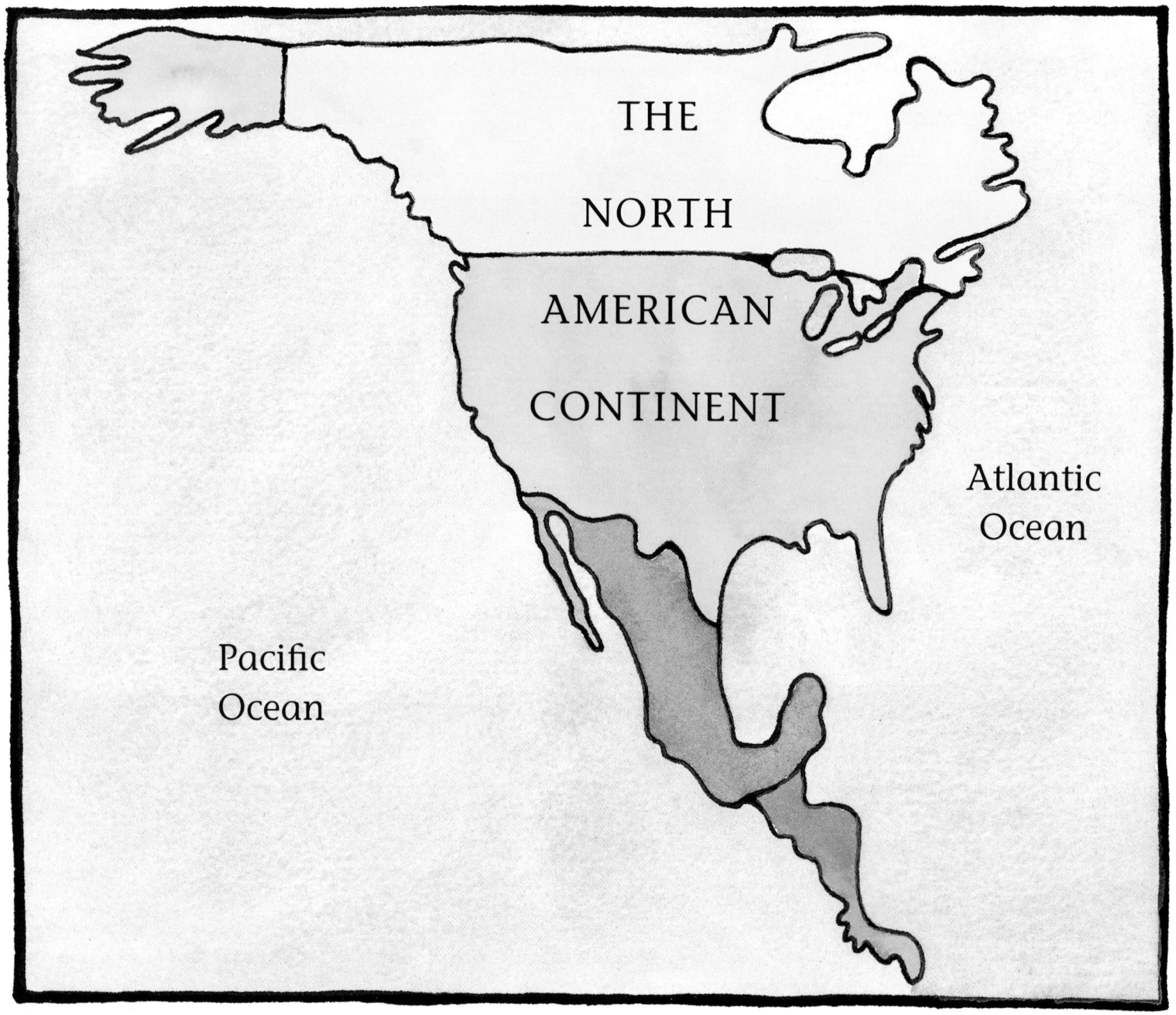

The biggest pieces of land on earth are continents.
Their shorelines meet the sea.

Islands are smaller pieces of land
that rise up out of the sea.

Some islands are born when volcanoes erupt below the sea. Hot lava cools, and over time it turns to soil where green things can grow.

Some islands are coral reefs that grow and grow
until they poke above the water,
and birds bring seeds to them.

Water gushing up from the ground, and rain,
and melted snow, fills streams, ponds, and lakes.

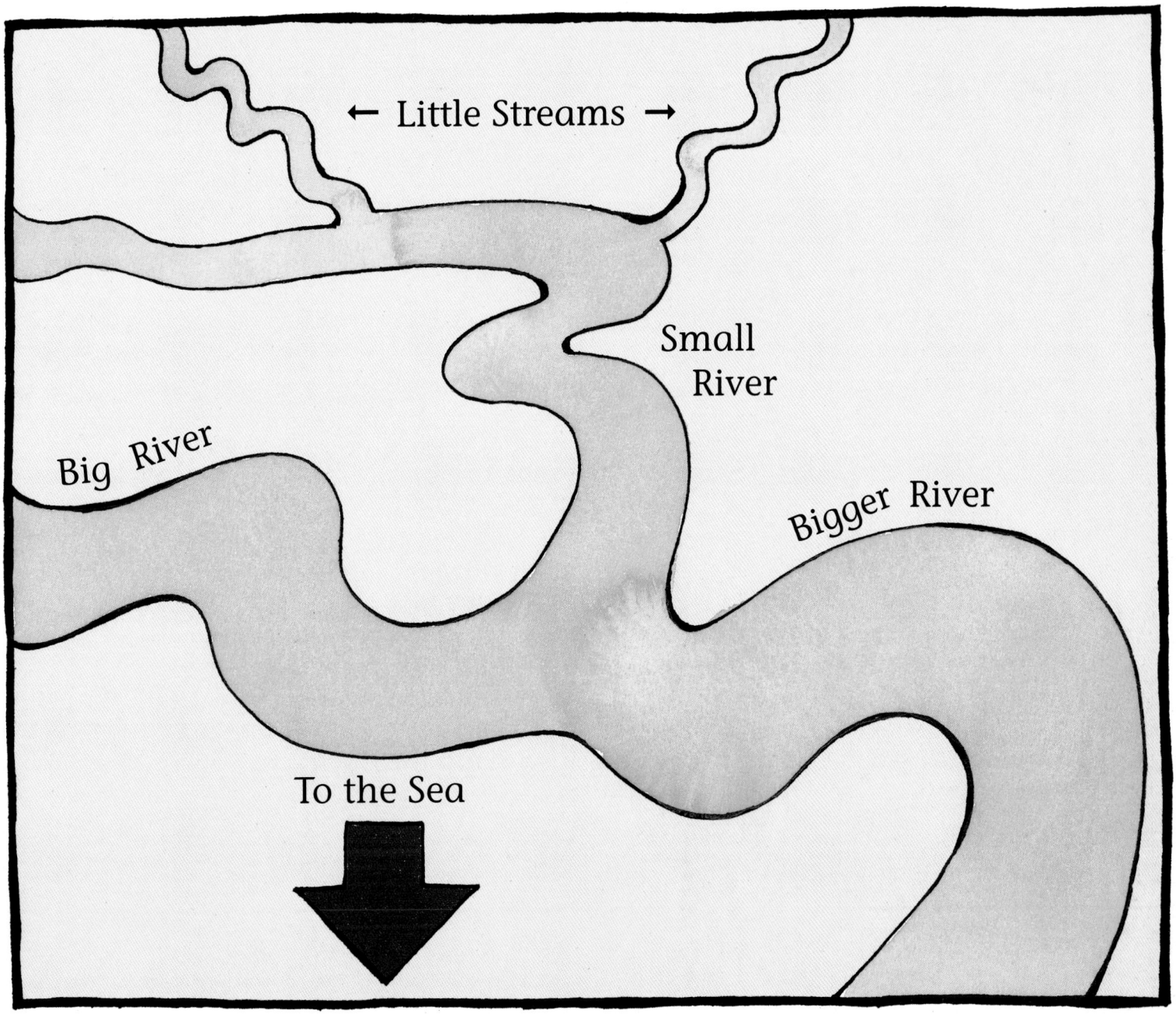

Streams flow into small rivers,
which flow into bigger ones.

Nothing can stop water from finding its way.

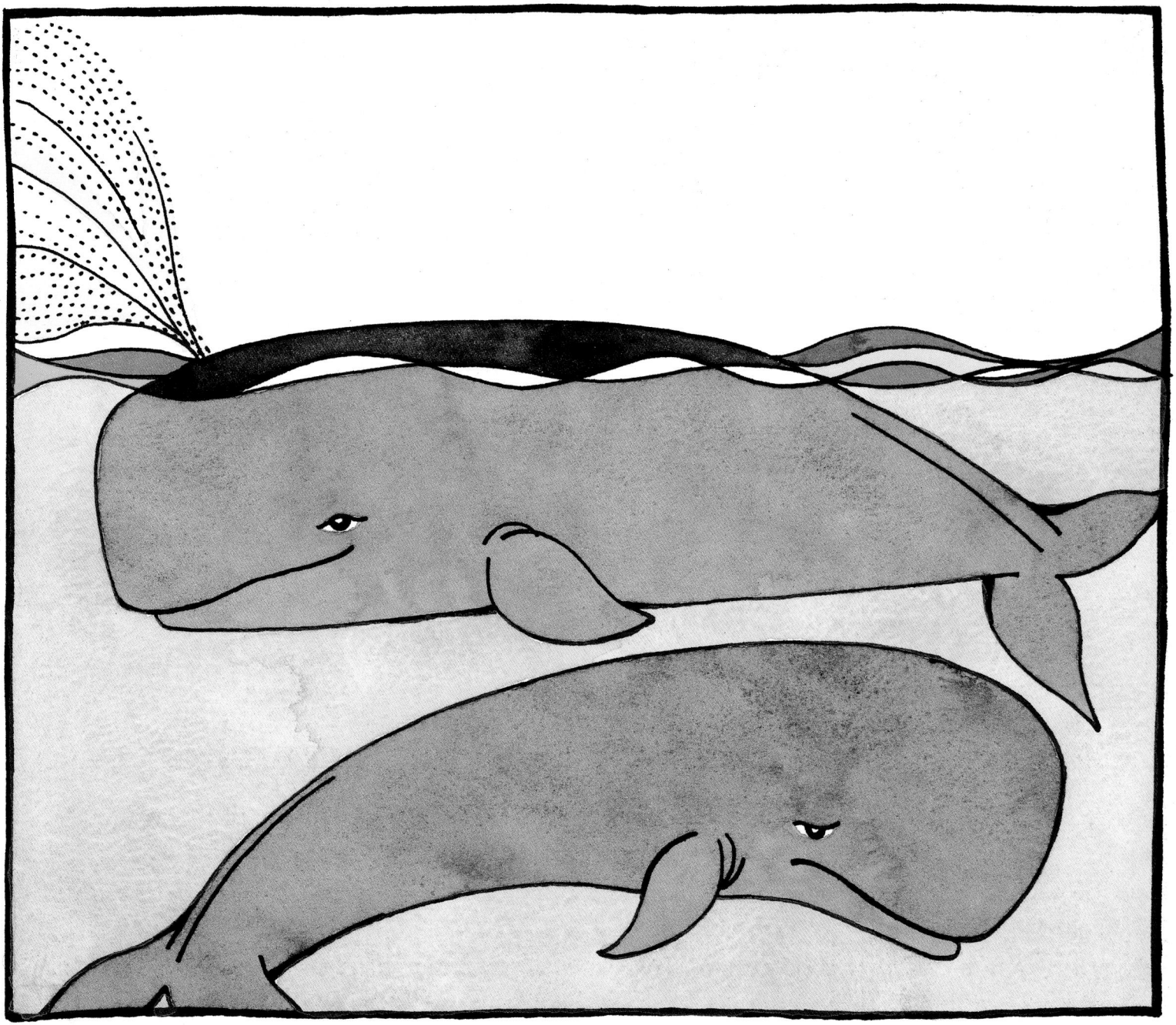

Some rivers dry up and stop flowing.
But some empty into the salty sea.

The land on our earth has rounded hills
that enclose green valleys.

There are many forests on our earth.
Rain forests are full of flowers, and birds,
and monkeys jumping through green-leafed trees.

There are hot, sandy deserts
where lizards live and prickly cacti grow.

There are dark, damp caves
that go far down into the earth.

There are tall canyons carved by years
and years of rushing water.

There are high, snowcapped mountains
reaching up to the clouds in the sky.

Our big, round earth is very beautiful.

It is my home and yours.

For
Christian Rockwell Brion

Copyright © 1998 by Anne Rockwell

All rights reserved. No part of this publication may be reproduced or transmitted in any form or by any means, electronic or mechanical, including photocopy, recording, or any information storage and retrieval system, without permission in writing from the publisher.

For information about permission to reproduce selections from this book, please write Permissions, Houghton Mifflin Harcourt Publishing Company, 215 Park Avenue South, NY, NY 10003.

www.hmhco.com

Library of Congress Cataloging-in-Publication Data
Rockwell, Anne F.
Our earth/Anne Rockwell.
p. cm.
Summary: A simple introduction to geography which explains such things as how the earth was shaped, how islands are born from volcanoes, and how gushing springs affect rivers.
1. Geography—Juvenile literature. [1. Geography.] I. Title.
G133.R63 1998
910—dc21 97-1247
ISBN 978-0-15-201679-1
ISBN 978-0-15-202383-6 pb

LEO 30 29 28 27 26 25 24 23 22
Printed in China
4500621561

The illustrations in this book were done in watercolor and gouache on paper.
The display type was set in Schwere.
The text type was set in Stone Informal.
Color separations by Tien Wah Press, Singapore
Production supervision by Stanley Redfern and Pascha Gerlinger
Designed by Linda Lockowitz